This book covers recent versions of any development tools and applications mentioned, but as technology changes the steps covered in this book may differ and vary slightly from version to version.

Please note that the author is in no way associated with or part of the developers of any of the third party development tools or applications mentioned within this book.

All names mentioned in this book and screenshots are included for informative purposes only. All information was to the authors knowledge correct at the time of writing, and no liability can be accepted for any inaccurate or out of date information that may exist. Mentions of any software or products do not represent an endorsement, and are only included for informative purposes. You should always make backups of your files before installing new software or changing settings.

If you have any comments, questions or suggestions for this book, e-mail the author at **simon@libraryplayer.co.uk** or visit their website at **www.libraryplayer.co.uk**

How to Develop Software

Table of Contents

Introduction

"I would never be able to learn how to develop software"

People say this to me frequently when I tell them what I do (developing software!) - I then try to explain that it is easier then they may think to learn about writing software. If you take logic from the real world (for example the steps involved to bake a cake) and apply it to giving instructions to your computer, it can seem a lot less daunting.

While most books these days focus on the language of the moment and particular development tools, I will be focusing on learning programming itself. This is why I've selected a language that has commands and statements similar to the English language, with a structure that is easier to apply to other languages.

Will this book teach you everything about software development within a few hours? Or make you an expert overnight? No, it won't, but hopefully it will give you a better idea of developing software, and give you a starting point to take things further if you wish.

I've also aimed this book at people who may not be interested in a career in software development, but just interested to learn more about it. For example, you may be a manager who hires developers, and want to learn a little bit more about the process, or you are just curious.

I also make heavy use of examples throughout the book to help illustrate and explain everything.

And don't worry if some of the things in this book seem a bit confusing – re-read chapters, and don't be scared to experiment and learn more about things that interest you.

Simon Pittman
23rd September 2015

What is software development?

Computers are stupid – they basically just do what we tell them to do (even if it does not always feel like that is true)!

Every piece of software you use on your computer, mobile phone or on the web will have been developed by someone using code, which has then been translated into a usable application.

Before we begin, a few things you should be aware of...

- This book will not make you into an expert software developer, but it will hopefully give you a good starting point, from which you can learn more if you wish.

- I will occasionally simplify some of the explanations and descriptions in this book, and will try to avoid going into technical detail or using jargon.

- Don't worry if you find any of the sections confusing – re-read the chapters, experiment and look up more information.

Programming Languages

Software is developed using code. There are many programming languages available that you can write code in, these include (but are not limited to)...

C	One of the oldest programming languages.
C++	Widely used and similar to C.
Java	Widely used, and available for different systems, its currently the default language used on Android phones.
ObjectiveC	Until recently, this was the widely used (and standard language) for developing software on Apple systems, including Macs and iPhones.
Swift	Apple's latest language, and fairly new, this is the current language of choice from Apple for developing on Apple based systems.
JavaScript	Not to be confused with Java, this language is used for writing code on web pages.
Visual Basic	A Microsoft language (inspired by the original BASIC language)
C#	C# is currently very popular and widely used, and is another language that originated from Microsoft.
COBOL	An old language, not as popular today, but can still occasionally see jobs advertised that use this language, as older applications on mainframes written using COBOL are still maintained to this day.
Fortran	Mainly used for scientific and mathematic applications.
Perl	Popular and widely used scripting language.
Python	Another widely used programming language.
Pascal	Originally intended for teaching programming, while not as widely used anymore it can be used for general application development. This is the language we will be using throughout this book.

This is not a complete list – there are many more languages out there, in fact if I listed every one, it could probably fill an entire book and more.

Many languages are for general use, but there are also specialist languages designed for particular areas, for example creating scientific or web applications.

In theory, once you learn one programming language, its fairly easy to learn others pretty quickly. Each language has their differences, but the logic and structure usually remains the same.

Stages of Software Development

There are several stages of software development – these can vary depending on who you're developing software for, your team, or which book you are reading!

In general, these are...

- **Analysis** – finding out what the software will actually do.
- **Design** – designing the software, how it will work, look, etc.
- **Implementation** – Writing the code for the software – this is what this book will primarily be covering.
- **Documentation** – documenting your code and application.
- **Testing** – making sure your software actually works the way its meant to work, and checking what happens if you enter any unexpected data. Your application may not be able to accept 0 as a value, but chances are that won't stop users attempting to do so.

Some methodologies follow a "waterfall" method, where once each stage is complete, you go to the next one, never returning to a previous stage. Other methods are more flexible, where you can go back to a previous stage, for example while testing you may wish to go back to the Design/Implementation stages.

There are numerous methodologies, approaches and different stages for managing software, however this is not a project management book, and we will focus on the coding (Implementation)!

Text Editors

You usually write your code using a text editor.

When I say text editor, I mean a text editor that only allows plain text – software such as Microsoft Word are word processors, not text editors, and should never be used for writing code!

An example of a text editor is Notepad that is included with Microsoft Windows.

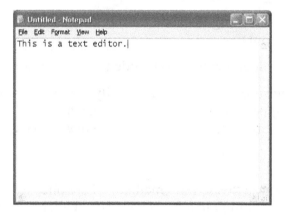

Some text editors are designed specifically for programming, and include options for **syntax highlighting** – this is when keywords, names, etc. are highlighted in different colours to make them more readable.

Compilers & Interpreters

Once you've written code, you need to be able to translate it into something that your computer will understand. There are two ways you can do this...

- **Interpreter** – common for web based languages, for example JavaScript – an interpreter reads the code line by line and runs the code as it reads it.

- **Compiler** – translates the code into an executable file which can then be run. Once code is compiled, you only need to distribute the executable file to people who will be using the application – they never need to see or have access to the code.

- Some languages and compilers (for example Java) also compile code into an intermediate executable file, which then requires another piece of software (similar to an interpreter) to run that intermediate file.

Most of the applications you use on the computer, including your office applications, text editors and even the operating system itself will have been compiled. You do not have a copy of the code for these applications – just the executable files to run the software. That is because the developer has **compiled** the application and created executable files that can run on your computer.

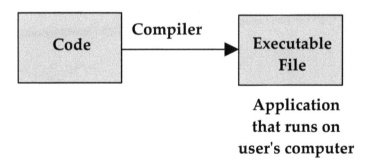

**Application
that runs on
user's computer**

More often then not, different companies will release their own versions of compilers for different languages. For example there are multiple compilers available for C++, C# and Pascal with different features and sometimes differences to the language.

Integrated Development Environment (IDE)

Integrated development environments (or IDEs for short) – sounds fancy and scary doesn't it?

Essentially, its a text editor, compiler and software development tools all rolled into one.

Many developers use an IDE for developing and coding, they can edit the text and compile the application from within the IDE.

An IDE will usually contain additional tools, including debugging, creating graphical user interfaces, testing, project management, working within a team and documenting code.

Examples of IDEs include...

- **Microsoft Visual Studio**
- **Eclipse**
- **Embarcadero RAD Studio**
- **Lazarus**
- **XCode**
- **MonoDevelop**
- **Xamarin**
- **NetBeans**

Some IDEs are available free of charge, while others require you to purchase a software license or subscription to use them.

Understanding Logic

Developing software involves understanding logic, describing exactly how you would carry out a task.

For example, if I was to describe how to serve some cornflakes for breakfast (for simplicity I'm already in the kitchen)...

Open cupboard door
Take out bowl
Put bowl on work surface
Grab box of cornflakes
Open box of cornflakes
Pour box of cornflakes into bowl, until bowl is half full
Stop pouring box of cornflakes
Close box of cornflakes
Put box of cornflakes away
Open fridge door
Remove milk from fridge
Open bottle of milk
Pour milk into bowl, until cornflakes third full
Stop pouring milk
Close bottle of milk
Put milk back in fridge
Grab spoon
Put spoon into bowl of cornflakes

Who knew that such a simple task would have so many steps? To simplify things much further, I have missed out steps like actually walking to the fridge, etc. but hopefully you'll still get the general idea.

Just like in developing software, the most minor of error can cause all sorts of problems!

Imagine if we missed out a step, or got a step wrong... we could end up serving too much cereal, spilling milk everywhere or break something!

In software development, its pretty much the same idea... you are telling the application exactly what to do, and how to do it. The code then gets translated into something the computer understands.

Another good example is directions on how to get to a place...

Go forward for 10 metres
Turn right
Go forward until you reach end of street
Turn left
Walk up hill until you reach halfway point

What would happen if there was a minor mistake in these directions? You would probably end up somewhere completely different!

What we'll be using

Before we begin...

First of all, a reminder that this book will not make you an expert, in fact it will only provide a starting point. Hopefully that starting point will help you take things further if you wish to be more involved in developing software, or scare you away which is also fine. If you don't want a career but you just want to learn a bit more about the software development process, then this book is for you.

I'm assuming you have the following skills...

- Comfortable with using a computer, including switching the computer on, using applications, etc.

- Knowing how to change basic settings, installing software, etc. is also going to be an advantage when reading this book.

- I'm assuming you don't know much about software development (which is why you've brought this book!) - but you may have a little idea about what it is.

- Willingness to learn!

Why Pascal?

For this book, the programming language we will be using Pascal. More specifically we shall be using the ObjectPascal dialect of Pascal (but to keep things simple we'll just refer to it as Pascal).

While today its used for general application development, when it was created in the 70s it was designed for teaching programming.

Pascal has a clean English-style syntax, for example **begin**, **end**, **write**, etc. which makes learning much easier.

You will often find that even with no programming knowledge, you can look at a piece of code (especially if its well written) and be able to understand what it is doing.

You'll be able to transfer the skills you learn from this book to other languages, for example while the C++, C# and Java languages are different, the structure is much the same.

While you can develop graphical applications in Pascal, we will focus command line applications in this book, allowing you to learn the very basics (and not be distracted about how something should look or adding buttons).

Obtaining & Installing Compiler

For this book, we will use the FreePascal compiler, available at:

www.freepascal.org

FreePascal is an open source (meaning anyone can view and modify the code within particular conditions) compiler for Pascal. FreePascal is itself written in Pascal – and the FreePascal compiler can even compile itself (i.e. the code for FreePascal can be compiled using FreePascal itself)!

Versions of FreePascal are available for different systems, including Windows, Apple Mac and Linux, so you will be able to download a version most appropriate for you.

Setting up your Text Editor

We will not use an IDE, but a simple text editor. This will allow you to focus on learning the language itself rather then a particular development environment.

We will use Notepad+ on Windows, which is available free of charge:

http://notepad-plus-plus.org/

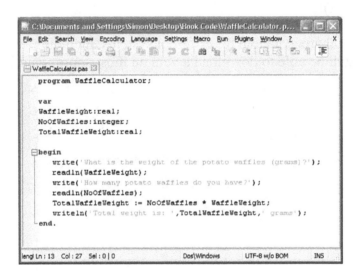

This text editor includes some features found in IDEs, for example syntax highlighting, without all the heavy features. If and when you develop applications commercially, you will most likely use a full development environment, however this book does not want to scare you away!

Using Your Text Editor & Saving Code

In your text editor, you can type your code, saving and making changes as you go along. When you save a file, it should have a meaningful and appropriate name, and end with ".pas" so the compiler and other applications know its a file containing Pascal code.

For example, if I created a VAT calculator, I may name the file **vatcalculator.pas**

You can then run the compiler separately to compile your code.

Using the FreePascal compiler

The following covers using Microsoft Windows, if you use another system you should check the documentation and help for your system!

The FreePascal compiler runs from the command line. In Windows, open a command prompt and go to the directory/folder containing your code. You can do this by typing:

cd foldername

Where foldername is the name of the directory/folder containing your code. Include any backslashes, and if you type in the start of a name and press the TAB key the command line will try to complete the rest of the name for you.

Once you install FreePascal, you can compile code by using the following command:

fpc filename

Obviously you'd substitute **filename** for the name of the file containing your code. An executable file will then be created in the same folder. You don't need to include the ".pas" at the end when typing in the command.

For example, to compile the VAT calculator example mentioned in the previous section, I would type:

fpc vatcalculator

If this feels too complicated and difficult, I suggest an alternative set of tools you can use in the next section.

If it seems too complicated so far

If you don't feel confident using the command line and a separate text editor (as covered in the previous two sections), or find it too difficult or confusing, you can use the Lazarus editor instead, which can be downloaded at:

lazarus.freepascal.org

Lazarus is an IDE that uses the FreePascal compiler.

When you run Lazarus, go to the **File** menu and select **New**.

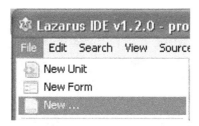

From the options that appear, select **Simple Program**.

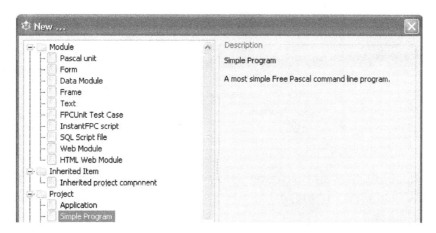

This will then create skeleton code, from which you can create your program. Don't let all the other options and windows in Lazarus put you off!

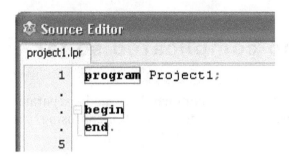

You do not need to change the **program** name in the text editor – when you save the file it will give the program a name that matches the filename (for example if you save as **vatcalculator** as the filename, the first line will change to **program vatcalculator**).

You will also notice that its put its own begin and end. for you you. You can then write your code.

You may wish to put a blank **readln;** statement at the end, this ensures when you are running your code in Lazarus you can see the last screen of text, and then just press enter to exit (if the last statement is just to display something, Lazarus will close the text window immediately afterwards so you can't see the last piece of text).

```
Source Editor
hello.lpr
1    program hello;
.
.    begin
.        writeln('Hello!');
5        readln;
.    end.
7
```

To run your code, click the run button on the Lazarus toolbar (it looks a bit like the play button that you'd find on a CD player).

All going well the application should run:

(In this example, its waiting for me to press enter due to the **readln** statement at the end, at which point the window will close).

If there are any error messages when compiling, they will appear in the **Messages** window at the bottom. You can double click an error to go to that line in the code.

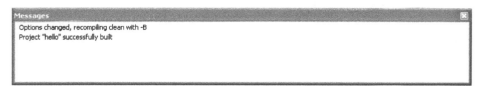

How this book works

- I'll be explaining each concept, idea or statement, and where possible will be including examples.

- Re-read chapters and go back/refer to previous sections if you get stuck.

- While you can read this book without typing in and trying the examples for yourself, I do encourage you to have a look at the code, type it in and run the examples, it can give you a better idea of how things work.

- Try out the examples – type them in and run them - and don't be scared to modify and experiment! The worst that can happen is that the code no longer compiles.

- It can take years and years to get to grips with software development – while this book won't make you an expert within a certain number of hours, it will hopefully give you an understanding and an introduction to software development, and hopefully help you find out more if you wish to take things further.

Basic structure

This is the basic structure of a Pascal program:

```
program programname;

begin

end.
```

At the start, you will see **program programname** - "programname" is the name of your application. You should aim to give a short, meaningful name, and the name should be within one word (i.e. no spaces) – if you wish to have more then one word, use uppercase letters to separate the words without spaces, for example **ProgramName**.

You will see that the end of the **program** statement includes a semi-colon, in Pascal (and many other languages) most statements end with a semicolon to indicate that it is the end of that current statement.

The **begin** and **end** keywords mark the beginning and end of your code, or statements. These do not have a semicolon since they are not actual statements (although anywhere else an **end** is used there will be a semicolon to indicate the end of those set of statements).

Note that the **end.** Statement has a full stop at the end – this indicates that its the end of the code.

When you save code, give it the name you have given in the **program** statement, in this example "programname.pas".

Indenting Code

You will see in my examples that I indent code.

Where possible, try to be consistent with the formatting of your code.

Many workplaces, groups and educational establishments will have their own standards, sometimes they are written down policies or guidelines.

In this book I've tried to stick to the following standard...

- Indenting of 3 spaces (i.e. pressing space 3 times) between **begin** and **end** statements.

- Indenting of 3 spaces after a new **procedure** or **function** is declared.

- Again, indenting of 3 spaces if a statement follows on from another statement, for example an **if** statement, **for** statement, etc.

- Don't worry if some of this does not make sense – it will do once I've covered the above statements. Also look at my examples to see how I've indented the code.

While Pascal is not strict when it comes to indenting, and whether statements are in uppercase, lower case, etc. be aware that other languages can be much stricter!

Hello World

Here's a very simple example to get started:

```
program hello;

begin
   writeln('Hello');
end.
```

You will notice that this program is called "hello". You will also see a new statement – **writeln**. This displays a piece of text on the screen. You will also notice that the **writeln** statement is indented by 3 spaces – this helps make the code more readable.

The **writeln** statement ends with a semicolon – marking the end of that statement.

Any text you wish to display must start and end with an apostrophe - ' - to indicate that it is a piece of text (or string).

Try typing this code yourself in Notepad+ (or Lazarus), and save the file as "hello.pas".

Try compiling the code by opening a command line window, going to the folder containing your code, and typing in the following command:

fpc hello

```
C:\Documents and Settings\Simon\Desktop>fpc hello
Free Pascal Compiler version 2.6.2 [2013/02/12] for i386
Copyright (c) 1993-2012 by Florian Klaempfl and others
Target OS: Win32 for i386
Compiling hello.pas
Linking hello.exe
4 lines compiled, 0.1 sec , 25504 bytes code, 1628 bytes data

C:\Documents and Settings\Simon\Desktop>
```

All going well, you should see something similar to the above, and no errors. If you do get any errors – don't panic! We will be coverings later in this book. Look at the error message that will appear – it will indicate which lines the errors occur. Check your code to see if it matches the above example – for example have you forgotten to include a semicolon at the end of the **writeln** statement?

Once your code compiles, you can run it by typing in the name of the application, in this example **hello**.

```
C:\Documents and Settings\Simon\Desktop>hello
Hello

C:\Documents and Settings\Simon\Desktop>
```

As you can see, it displays a simple "Hello" message – and that's about it. May not seem very exciting but all going well you will have just written your first application!

Feel free and don't be scared to experiment, changing the Hello message to something else, or even adding additional **writeln** statements!

Comments

You can add comments to your code, you may wish to add comments to...

- Help make it easier to understand what particular sections of code do – useful if other people will look at your code in the future, or to remind yourself of what something does.

- Including information about who wrote the code, copyright, what the application does, version numbering, etc. at the top of the code file.

- When checking for errors or removing a line from code, it is sometimes a good idea to comment out the line of code rather then deleting it, especially if there may be unexpected results from deleting the line or you only wish to remove the line of code temporarily.

In Pascal, comments start with a opening curly bracket and end with a closing curly bracket, for example:

```
{this is a comment}
```

Comments are completely ignored by the compiler, they basically treat comments as if they don't exist.

Let's look at the hello world example again with comments included:

```
program hello;
{by Simon Pittman
Displays a simple hello message.}

begin
   writeln('Hello');    {displays the message}
end.
```

At the top, I've included a comment with my name (to indicate that I wrote the code!) and also what the application does.

For the **writeln** statement I've included a comment indicating what that line of code does. This is an extreme example really – I wouldn't usually include a comment for every line of code, or for something as simple as a **writeln** statement, but it does illustrate how useful comments can be.

When you are carrying out complex calculations, drawing items on the screen, etc. comments can be very useful for helping to explain what you are doing.

I've modified our hello example a bit, to comment out a line of code:

```
program hello;
{by Simon Pittman
Displays a simple hello message.}

begin
{   writeln('Hello');}
end.
```

If you compile the above code (try it for yourself) the application won't actually do anything, since the only line of code is now commented out. In more complex applications, you may find temporarily commenting out code useful for identifying causes of errors, or temporarily deleting lines of code.

Variables, Constants & Data Types

Variables

When writing code, you will sometimes need to store a value or data in memory. You can do this using variables. You can declare a variable using the **var** statement.

Let's have a look at the following example...

```
program SayHello;
{by Simon Pittman
Displays a personalised hello message to the user.}

var
UsersName:string;

begin
   write('What is your name?');
   readln(UsersName);
   writeln('Hello ',UsersName,'!');
end.
```

You will see between the **program** and **begin** lines the **var** section, declaring your variables. You should try to give your variables meaningful names – for example the variable declared above stores the users name.

You will see that variables are declared with the name of the variable, followed by a colon (:) and then the data type. You can have multiple variables in the **var** section.

Type in the above code yourself, compile and run.

```
C:\Documents and Settings\Simon\Desktop\Book Code>sayhello
What is your name?Simon
Hello Simon!

C:\Documents and Settings\Simon\Desktop\Book Code>
```

Obviously unless your name is Simon (or you pretend your name is Simon), you will see a different hello message!

Data Types

The previous section used a **string** data type in the example to store the users name. There are different types of data that you can use:

Data type	Description
String	Stores text – strings can usually contain up to 255 characters.
Char	A single character.
Integer	A number without decimals.
Smallint	A number without decimals, but usually a smaller range of numbers then available in Integer (and therefore takes up less memory).
Boolean	Stores true/false.
Real	Storing floating point numbers with decimals.

There are other data types available, and the names can vary depending on which language you use, but the above are the most common ones that you will probably use to begin with!

The amount of memory that different types of data can occupy can vary.

Assigning values to variables

In addition to storing values in variables from user input, you can also assign a value directly. If variables contain numeric values you can carry out calculations with them. For example, to add two numbers:

```
TotalNumbers := FirstNumber + SecondNumber;
```

Note the colon and equals (:=) - this means you are assigning a value to the variable. Even experienced developers sometimes make the mistake in Pascal of just using an equals sign (Pascal uses the equals - = - on its own for comparing values, and the equals with a colon - := - for assigning values).

If you try the above with string values, it will combine the two strings together rather then add the values (for example if you had two strings with "Simon" and "Pittman" the result would be "SimonPittman").

Remember the semicolon at the end as well to mark the end of the statement.

Constants

The values of variables can change – which is why they are called variables (their values vary)!

Sometimes you will want to store a value in memory, but have that item remain the same. That's what constants are for. For example...

- Having a value that does not change but used throughout your code.
- Setting the length of something.

With a constant, its easier to modify the code and change values in the future just by modifying that one line of code. It can also help to make your code more readable.

Constant declarations go before variable declarations, and are declared in the following format:

```
const
ConstantName = value;
```

Obviously you would substitute **ConstantName** and **value** with the name and value of the constant. You do not need to enter a data type, and you just use the = symbol rather then ":=" to set the value.

Like variables you can have more then one constant declaration...

**const
FirstConstantName = FirstValue;
SecondConstantName = SecondValue;**

Once a constant is declared, you can use it as you would a variable (apart from within code that would attempt to change the value).

Unlike variables, you can not change the values of constants within your code (they remain constant throughout). If you try to change the value of a constant, the code won't compile and the compiler will display an error.

The best way to explain this is with another example...

```
program vatcalculator;
{by Simon Pittman
Calculates the amount of VAT and total price on an item.}

const
VATRate = 0.17;

var
ItemPrice:real;
ItemVAT:real;
TotalPrice:real;

begin
    write('What is the price?');
    readln(ItemPrice);
    ItemVAT := ItemPrice * VATRate;
    TotalPrice := ItemPrice + ItemVAT;
    writeln('Amount of VAT: ',ItemVAT);
    writeln('Price inc. VAT: ',TotalPrice);
end.
```

In the above example, I've stored the VAT rate as a constant, as this value will not change. If the government ever change the rate of VAT, I just need to modify one line of code and recompile it![1]

Type in the above code yourself, compile it and try out the software.

---

[1]In a real world applcation, the VAT rate would probably be stored in a settings file, and the application would then read that settings file and store the VAT rate into a variable. However this example hopefully still gives you a good example of how constants can be useful!

```
C:\Documents and Settings\Simon\Desktop\Book Code>vatcalculator.exe
What is the price?2.50
Amount of VAT:   4.250000000000000E-001
Price inc. VAT:   2.925000000000000E+000

C:\Documents and Settings\Simon\Desktop\Book Code>_
```

Try running the application a few times, entering different prices.

Also experiment and try the following with the code...

- Change the VAT rate a few times (unfortunately changing the VAT rate in your application does not force the government to change the rate in the real world!), recompile the code and try the application.

- When running the application and prompted for the price – try entering letters and symbols (including the pound symbol). The application crashes and you see a runtime error! More on errors later on in the book.

Global and Local Variables/Constants

The variables we have seen in this chapter are known as **global variables**. This is because the variables and constants are available for use throughout your application.

Later in the book we will learn more about **local variables and constants**, which can only be used and accessed within a particular section of your code.

Meaningful Names

When thinking of names for your variables, constants or anything else, try to give them a meaningful name, that will help you and anyone else looking at your code understand what it does.

For example, **VATRate** may be a more meaningful name then **rate** or even **x**. **Password** can be a more meaningful name then **p**.

Keep them short if you can – but don't worry if it looks too long (within reason!) - as long as it makes your code more readable. You can use a mixture of uppercase and lowercase letters to help separate words, for example **PersonsName**.

When developing applications commercially, most modern development tools have auto completion in their editors, to save typing in long names.

I've seen some developers use just a single letter for variable names, but then get confused and forget later on when they look at their code – meaningful names can prevent this problem.

Displaying & User Input

User Input

Pretty much every application needs the user to input data of some description.

In a graphical application, this can be by clicking buttons, entering text, etc.

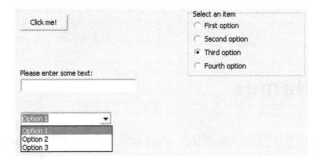

When writing a command line application in Pascal, we get user input using the **readln** statement:

```
readln(VariableName);
```

Replace VariableName with the name of a variable that will store the data the user inputs.

You will have seen this statement used in previous sections, including the hello application that asked for the user's name and the VAT calculator.

You can have a string variable (a piece of text) or a number – however if you have a variable that is one of the number data types and the user enters a piece of text, then the application will crash!

Here's another example:

```
program AddNumbers;

var
FirstNumber,SecondNumber:integer;
TotalNumber:integer;

begin
   write('Enter the first number:');
   readln(FirstNumber);
   write('Enter the second number:');
   readln(SecondNumber);
   TotalNumber := FirstNumber + SecondNumber;
   writeln('The total is ',TotalNumber);
end.
```

Before I explain the above example, looking at the code, can you guess? Answer: it gets the user to enter two numbers, adds them together and displays the total.

Type in the above example yourself, save it (remember the filename will be "AddNumbers.pas") and compile it.

```
C:\Documents and Settings\Simon\Desktop\Book Code>AddNumbers
Enter the first number:5
Enter the second number:2
The total is 7
```

When you run the example, enter a few different numbers, and see which totals it displays. Run the application a few times, and use different numbers.

Here's a challenge for you – try running the application a few times and attempt the following...

- Enter numbers with decimal values (e.g. **4.23**)
- Type in some letters instead of numbers (e.g. **S**, etc.)

```
C:\Documents and Settings\Simon\Desktop\Book Code>AddNumbers
Enter the first number:4.23
Runtime error 106 at $0040142D
  $0040142D
  $00406E91
```

```
C:\Documents and Settings\Simon\Desktop\Book Code>AddNumbers
Enter the first number:8
Enter the second number:nine
Runtime error 106 at $00401482
  $00401482
  $00406E91
```

You'll notice when you type in something that is not an integer value (e.g. a number with a decimal, a letter, etc.) the application will crash, producing a run time error. We will have a look at checking the application for errors later in the book – remember its important to choose the correct data type for your requirements, and to ensure your application checks for errors.

Finally, just for fun, run the application again and use a negative number (e.g. -5) instead of a positive number and see what happens.

```
C:\Documents and Settings\Simon\Desktop\Book Code>AddNumbers
Enter the first number:-5
Enter the second number:10
The total is 5
```

Don't be scared to modify the code:

- Try substituting the integer data types with a **real** data type instead - when you do this you will notice it will now accept decimal values.

```
Enter the first number:2.55
Enter the second number:1.20
The total is  3.75000000000000E+000
```

- Substitute the data types with a **string** instead of an **integer**. You will find the application behaves very strangely, combining the two numbers rather then adding them. This is because when handling strings, **TotalNumber := FirstNumber + SecondNumber** statement will combine two strings together into a single string rather then adding two numbers together.

```
Enter the first number:4
Enter the second number:3
The total is 43
```

- Always consider the most appropriate data types for variables – this is important for accuracy, memory consumption, etc.

Don't just read this and take my word with the above examples and explanations – spend some time trying them out yourself. Modify your code, and see what happens.

Displaying Data

In every example so far, we have used the **writeln** and **write** statements to display information to the user. What are the differences between these two statements?

writeln	Writes the information to the screen and then goes to a new line.
write	Writes the information to the screen and stays at the current line – particularly useful when prompting for user input.

Usually, we'd write to the screen in the following way:

```
writeln('A piece of text');
```

This would write "A piece of text" to the screen. Note the apostrophe at the start and end, which identify this as a string and writes that to the screen.

If you are writing a number to the screen, you won't need to include an apostrophe (although you will very rarely use the following example):

```
writeln(2)
```
– this would write the number 2 to the screen.

2

You can also write the value of a variable or constant to the screen (whether is an Integer, Real or String data type):

```
writeln(VariableName);
```

This would write the value of VariableName to the screen. You will notice that apostrophes are not used as these are variable names.

You can also write a combination of text and variable values to the screen by separating with a comma, for example:

```
writeln('The value is: ',VariableName);
```

If VariableName was a string containing "Bananas" as its value, it would write "The value is: Bananas" to the screen.

This may all sound a bit confusing – read this section so far a few times, and also have a look at the examples in previous chapters which help illustrate this. Don't worry, it will hopefully come to you in time!

The best way to explain this is with another example!

```
program WaffleCalculator;

var
WaffleWeight:real;
NoOfWaffles:integer;
TotalWaffleWeight:real;

begin
    writeln('What is the weight of the potato waffles (grams)?');
    readln(WaffleWeight);
    writeln('How many potato waffles do you have?');
    readln(NoOfWaffles);
    TotalWaffleWeight := NoOfWaffles * WaffleWeight;
    writeln('Total weight is: ',TotalWaffleWeight,' grams');
end.
```

Once again, before I reveal what the above example does, look at the code and see if you can figure out what it does for yourself. Where possible, well written code should be easy to read, even by someone with little software development skills!

This application calculates the total weight of a number of potato waffles, based on the weight of a single potato waffle[2].

Type the above code and save (remember to save it as "WaffleCalculator.pas").

Compile and run the application:

```
C:\Documents and Settings\Simon\Desktop\Book Code>fpc WaffleCalculator
Free Pascal Compiler version 2.6.2 [2013/02/12] for i386
Copyright (c) 1993-2012 by Florian Klaempfl and others
Target OS: Win32 for i386
Compiling WaffleCalculator.pas
Linking WaffleCalculator.exe
14 lines compiled, 0.1 sec , 33344 bytes code, 1916 bytes data

C:\Documents and Settings\Simon\Desktop\Book Code>WaffleCalculator
What is the weight of the potato waffles (grams)?
7
How many potato waffles do you have?
10
Total weight is:  7.00000000000000E+001 grams
```

As usual, run the application a few times and enter different values.

---

[2]Thank you to Mubasher Choudry at Mubasher Choudry Family Law Solutions in Aberdeen who suggested that I include an example referring to potato waffles.

See what happens when you enter an unusual value (or enter kg or grams after entering the weight – the application crashes).

```
C:\Documents and Settings\Simon\Desktop\Book Code>WaffleCalculator
What is the weight of the potato waffles (grams)?9grams
Runtime error 106 at $0040142D
  $0040142D
  $00408351
```

You will notice this example uses a **writeln** statement, and when you type in text its below that prompt. Lets substitute the first two **writeln** statements with the **write** statement:

```pascal
program WaffleCalculator;

var
WaffleWeight:real;
NoOfWaffles:integer;
TotalWaffleWeight:real;

begin
   write('What is the weight of the potato waffles
(grams)?');
   readln(WaffleWeight);
   write('How many potato waffles do you have?');
   readln(NoOfWaffles);
   TotalWaffleWeight := NoOfWaffles * WaffleWeight;
   writeln('Total weight is: ',TotalWaffleWeight,' grams');
end.
```

Compile and run the modified code...

```
C:\Documents and Settings\Simon\Desktop\Book Code>WaffleCalculator
What is the weight of the potato waffles (grams)?5.5
How many potato waffles do you have?10
Total weight is:  5.50000000000000E+001 grams
```

You will notice that when you enter the weight and number of waffles, these appear on the same line as the prompt – which look a lot clearer and tidier!

The line that displays the total weight is a good example of mixing different values together (e.g. displaying text and the value of a variable:

```
writeln('Total weight is: ',TotalWaffleWeight,' grams');
```

When viewing the results of calculations always check the calculations yourself to be sure they are producing the correct results! **A calculation result may be displayed – but is it the correct result?**

Try modifying the code for yourself, for example...

- You could store the weight of potato waffles in a constant (as covered in a previous section) instead of prompting the user each time you run the application – in a real world application this value would probably be saved to file and stored as a setting.

- How much do the potato waffles cost? You could include the price per potato waffle or price per weight, and calculate and display the price in addition to calculating/displaying the total weight.

Be brave – try creating an application yourself from scratch using what you've learned so far. Here is an idea:

- Get the user to input the total weight of a coin bag, and calculate the total number of coins in the bag based on the weight of a single coin (hint: set the weight of a coin as a constant, and use the / for divisions).

It may help to work out how to do the above on paper first before you type in any code.

Procedures & Functions

When developing software, it can make sense to split and break your code/logic down into smaller steps. You may also wish to make it easier to reuse code and carry out the same task more then once.

For example, if you where creating a shopping cart application, you might want to split the requirements as follows:

- Get the customer orders
- Display the total prices plus postage
- Confirm order with customer
- Process payment
- Send the customer a receipt
- Display confirmation message

You could then split the above into smaller steps, for example:

- **Get the customer orders**
  - Select products and update cart
  - Check stock availability
- **Display the total prices plus postage**
- **Confirm order with customer**
- **Process payment**
  - Validate customer payment details
  - Update product inventory
- **Send the customer a receipt**
  - E-mail customer receipt
  - E-mail order handling department so they can process order
- **Display confirmation message**

Not only does this help make a complex application seem less complex, but it can also help make your code reusable. For example, you may wish to reuse the payment processing code for an application that processes employee's payments.

Another advantage is that it makes working on complex applications within a team much easier. For example one team member may work on the order confirmation, while other team members focus on the payment processing. They will create and test their code independently, and then combine their code to create the single application.

If the idea behind this still sounds complicated, imagine building a car – the car is made of different components, for example a motor, seats, etc. all of which are manufactured separately – these different "components" of the car are then combined to create a car. Different car parts can not only be used in a car currently being built, but other cars and even other forms of transport!

In Pascal, there are two ways of splitting your code into modules – **procedures** and **functions**.

Procedures

Procedures can be a bit like a mini program, with similar declarations.

For example, if you wanted to create an application that gets two numbers from the user and then display the total, you could split this as follows:

- Getting the user to enter the numbers.
- Add the numbers and display the total.

And here is the code...

```
program ProcedureExample;

var
FirstNumber,SecondNumber:integer;

procedure GetNumbersFromUser;
{gets the user to enter the numbers}

   begin    {procedure}
      write('Enter the first number:');
       readln(FirstNumber);
       write('Enter the second number:');
       readln(SecondNumber);
   end;    {procedure}

function CalculateTotal:integer;
{adds both numbers and returns the total}

   begin    {function}
      CalculateTotal := FirstNumber + SecondNumber;
   end;    {function}

procedure DisplayTotal;
{adds the two numbers together and displays
```

```
the total}

    var
    TotalNumbers:integer;

    begin    {procedure}
       TotalNumbers :=
CalculateTotal(FirstNumber,SecondNumber);
       writeln('The total is ',TotalNumbers);
    end;    {procedure}

begin
    GetNumbersFromUser;
    DisplayTotal;
end.
```

Declaring a **procedure** is similar to declaring a **program** – in some ways you can imagine it as a program within a program! Or creating your own command/statement – in fact some of the commands/statements within the language are actually just built-in procedures/functions.

A procedure has its own **begin** and **end;** with the relevant code going in between (note for procedures the **end** has a semi-colon after it).

Try to give the procedure a relevant name, reflecting what it does. After the procedure is declared, you will notice I like to add a short comment explaining what it does in a bit more detail.

I like to add a comment after the **begin** and **end** for the procedure to help identify it as the begin and end for a procedure, however this is not essential and most developers I know don't do this!

In the second procedure, **DisplayTotal**, you will notice it has its own variable declaration – this is known as a local variable, as the variable is only used and available within that procedure. In this example, a local variable is used to display the total.

It is also possible to declare constants within a procedure or function.

To call a procedure within the application, just enter the procedure name as a statement (with any parameters in brackets – more on parameters shortly), e.g.

DisplayTotal;

You can call procedures and functions from other procedures/functions or within the main program code.

As usual try compiling and running the example yourself a few times, and use different numbers (and even some unexpected values!)

```
C:\Documents and Settings\Simon\Desktop\Book Code>ProcedureExample
Enter the first number:5
Enter the second number:4
The total is 9
```

Parameters

Both procedures and functions can have parameters, these are variables passed to it that it can use.

What are the advantages of parameters rather then just using global variables?

- It makes the procedure/function more reusable.
- You can use the procedure/function with different variables.
- Reduces the chance of errors caused by just using global variables (e.g. incorrectly setting and changing a value).

Let's look at an example...

```
program ProcedureExample;

var
FirstNumber,SecondNumber:integer;

procedure GetNumbersFromUser(VAR
FirstNumber,SecondNumber:integer);
{gets the user to enter the numbers}

   begin    {procedure}
     write('Enter the first number:');
      readln(FirstNumber);
      write('Enter the second number:');
      readln(SecondNumber);
   end;    {procedure}

function CalculateTotal(CONST
FirstNumber,SecondNumber:integer):integer;
{adds both numbers and returns the total}

   begin    {function}
```

```
        CalculateTotal := FirstNumber + SecondNumber;
    end;    {function}

procedure DisplayTotal(CONST
FirstNumber,SecondNumber:integer);
{adds the two numbers together and displays
the total}

    var
    TotalNumbers:integer;

    begin    {procedure}
       TotalNumbers :=
CalculateTotal(FirstNumber,SecondNumber);
        writeln('The total is ',TotalNumbers);
    end;    {procedure}

begin
    GetNumbersFromUser(FirstNumber,SecondNumber);
    DisplayTotal(FirstNumber,SecondNumber);
end.
```

This is a modified version of the previous example, where we add two numbers.

You can have any number of parameters, and they can be any data type.

If they have a **VAR** the parameters can be changed within the procedure/function. In the above example its illustrated in the GetNumbersFromUser procedure, as the values of those parameters change as a result of the user entering their numbers.

```
procedure GetNumbersFromUser(VAR
FirstNumber,SecondNumber:integer);
```

If a parameter has a **CONST** at the start, it will not change within the procedure – it is read only.

```
function CalculateTotal(CONST
FirstNumber,SecondNumber:integer);
```

You can have a parameter without a **VAR** or **CONST** declaration – these parameters can be changed within the procedure/function but any changes will be discarded outside the procedure/function – imagine it as similar to creating a local variable with the parameters values discarded at the end and reset to their original values.

Parameters of different types must be seperated with a semi-colon (;)

Procedures and functions with parameters are called by including the appropriate variables in brackets.

```
GetNumbersFromUser(firstNum,secondNum);
TotalNumbers := CalculateTotal(first,second);
```

When calling procedures/functions with parameters they can be any variable, provided its the same data type. This makes the code reusable, for example you might wish to use a function within another application, or use a function multiple times to carry out the same calculations with different variables.

Functions

Functions allow you to write a module of code that returns a result/value – this can be useful for carrying out calculations.

In the previous example, we saw the **CalculateTotal** example:

```
function CalculateTotal(CONST
FirstNumber,SecondNumber:integer):integer;
{adds both numbers and returns the total}

   begin    {function}
      CalculateTotal := FirstNumber + SecondNumber;
   end;    {function}
```

This is different from a procedure in that it returns a value – the type of which is specified at the end of the function declaration.

To declare a function, you use the **function** keyword, followed by the function's name, any parameters, and then a colon and data type for the value that is returned:

function FunctionName(CONST ParameterName:ParameterType):ReturnType

When you are ready to return the value to be returned, use the function name and assign a value to it (see the above CalculateTotal example):

FunctionName := ValueToBeReturned

Once a value is returned, the function exits – so if you return a value halfway through the function then the remaining statements will not run!

To call a function, use the function name and any parameters, similar to how you would call a procedure. Unlike procedures, functions can be used within a statement. For example:

VariableName := FunctionName(ParameterName);

would set VariableName to the value returned in a function.

```
if IsListEmpty(TheList) then
    writeln('List empty!')
else
    writeln('Has items');
```

would use a function of a boolean variable type to check whether a list of items is empty, and then carry out the appropriate actions.

If you have a long **if** statement with lots of **or** and **and**s it may be easier to split them into a separate function and then just have the if statement call that function!

In the CalculateTotal example, the function is called as follows:

```
TheTotal := CalculateTotal(4,5);
```

In this example, TheTotal would store the number 9, which would be the result of the CalculateTotal function.

Local Constants & Variables

So far, when we have wished to store a value in memory, we have used **global variables**. This is because the variables can be seen and used throughout that program.

Local variables are variables that are declared within a procedure or function, and can only be seen and used by that procedure/function. For example, you may wish to temporarily store values in memory while the procedure/function is running.

When the procedure or function has finished running, all memory used by that variable is cleared – the variable can not be used anywhere else within the application.

Global variables are declared outside the procedure/functions and are therefore visible throughout that code file, and can be used within procedures, functions and the main program code.

Let's look at this procedure:

```
procedure DisplayTotal(CONST FirstNumber,SecondNumber:integer);
{adds the two numbers together and displays
the total}

   var
   TotalNumbers:integer;

   begin    {procedure}
      TotalNumbers := CalculateTotal(FirstNumber,SecondNumber);
        writeln('The total is ',TotalNumbers);
   end;    {procedure}
```

The **TotalNumbers** variable is a **local variable** – it is declared within the procedure and can only be used within it. Once a procedure has finished (i.e. it reaches the **end;**) any memory used by the **TotalNumbers** variable is cleared.

At the top of the example in the Procedures section, the start of the code file looked like this...

```
program ProcedureExample;

var
FirstNumber,SecondNumber:integer;
```

Both **FirstNumber** and **SecondNumber** are **global variables** – they can be accessed throughout the program, by procedures, functions and the main program code. They can read the values and change them.

However if you do use global variables within a procedure or function, I suggest you use parameters and pass the values through the parameters, so the procedure/function can be reused and reduce the risk of errors.

Making Decisions

At some point your application may have to make a decision – for example...

- Ask the user to make a selection, and then carry out the appropriate action.

- Check what the user has entered is valid, and then either proceed or stop and warn the user.

- Carry out a calculation depending on the result of another calculation.

If statements

The simplest form of decision making within developing software is the if statement – pretty much every language has this statement (although how you use it can differ).

If a certain condition is met, then the next statement will be carried out, otherwise it is ignored.

if variablename = true then
  Carry out statement;

You can also carry out a block of statements by using **begin** and **end;**

if variablename = true then
  begin
    Statement 1
    Statement 2
    etc.
  end;

You can also have an optional **else** as part of the if statement – so if the condition is not met then the statement that comes after **else** is carried out.

if variablename = true then
  Carry out statement
else
  Carry out this statement instead;

When using the **else** the statement that comes after the **if** (i.e. the statement between the **if** and **else**) does not have a semicolon at the end – this is because the whole **if...else...** and the statements to carry out if the condition is/is not met are considered one statement.

If you have a block of statements (i.e. statements between **begin** and **end**) then the **end** does not need a semicolon:

```
if variablename = true then
  begin
    Statement 1;
    Statement 2;
    etc.
  end   {notice there is no semicolon here!}
else
  Carry out statement;
```

You can also have a block of statements for the **else** statements:

```
if variablename = true then
  begin
    Statement 1;
    Statement 2;
    etc.
  end
else
  begin
    Statement 1;
    Statement 2;
    etc.
  end;
```

Remember if you have a lot of statements between a **begin** and **end;** block of code, it may be simpler and make the code a bit more readable if you move those statements to a separate procedure/function.

And here's one of my examples:

```
program TaxCalculator;
```

```
const
TaxRate = 0.10;    {tax rate for every pound}
MinimumEarnings = 2000;    {earnings before tax paid}

var
EmployeesIncome:real;

procedure DisplayTax(const EmployeesIncome:real);

   var
   TaxToPay:real;
   PayWithTaxDeducted:real;

   begin    {procedure}
      TaxToPay := EmployeesIncome * TaxRate;
       PayWithTaxDeducted := EmployeesIncome - TaxToPay;
       writeln('Tax to pay: ',TaxToPay);
       writeln('Income with tax deducted: ',PayWithTaxDeducted);
   end;    {procedure}

begin
   write('What is your employees income?');
   readln(EmployeesIncome);
   if EmployeesIncome >= MinimumEarnings then
      DisplayTax(EmployeesIncome)
   else
      writeln('They don''t need to pay any tax!');
end.
```

Have a look at the example and what it does – more importantly type it in and try it out yourself.

The example gets the user to enter an employee's income, and then determines whether they need to pay tax, and how much.

The **if** statement in the above code calculates and displays the tax details (I've decided to put the code in a separate procedure to make it easier to read), otherwise it tells the user they don't need to pay any tax!

You can also have an if statement within another if statement – this is known as a **nested if statement**:

```
if condition = true then
  if another condition = true then
    Carry out action;
```

You could however reach a point where your code becomes really long:

```
if condition = true then
  if another condition = true then
    if third condition = true then
      carry out action
    else
      if this condition = true then
        carry out another action
      else
        carry out this action instead;
```

The above example is definitely more unreadable and slightly confusing! We shall look at alternatives to the if statement very shortly.

You can have more then one condition in the if statement:

```
if (first condition = true) or (second condition = true) then
  carry out action;
```

In the above code, if either (but not necessarily both) conditions are true then the action is carried out. You can also use an **and**:

```
if (first condition = true) and (second condition = true) then
  carry out action;
```

Both conditions must be true to carry out the appropriate action. You can also mix and match, and use both **or** and **and** in the same if statement – but make sure your code doesn't become unreadable and confusing – it may be more appropriate to use a function instead or nested if statements.

You can also use the in keyword to check if a variable has more then one possible value:

```
if VariableName in[5,6,7] then
    writeln('Is one of the numbers');
```

The above example writes "Is one of the numbers" to the screen if VariableName has the value of either 5, 6 or 7. This is similar to using an **or** but can be less complicated and easier to read!

Case statements

Sometimes you may wish to make a decision based on the value of a particular variable – and have multiple decisions. For example, selecting a menu option,

You could use multiple nested if statements:

```
if UsersSelection = 1 then
   writeln('First option selected')
else
   if UsersSelection = 2 then
      writeln('Second option selected')
   else
      if UsersSelection = 3 then
         writeln('Third option selected')
      else
         if UsersSelection = 4 then
            writeln('Fourth option selected')
       else
            writeln('No option selected!');
```

As you can see, this makes the code really long, and can look a bit messy! What if you need to add an additional selection (and therefore an additional if statement) in the future? What if you have many selections (you could spend an awful lot of time writing if statements!)?

The **case** statement allows you to make more then one decision based on a value.

```
case VariableName of
   1 : writeln('First option selected');
   2 : writeln('Second option selected');
   3 : writeln('Third option selected');
```

```
    4 : writeln('Fourth option selected');
else
    writeln('No option selected!');
end;
```

As you can see, the above is much easier to read. Its also easier to update and make changes to the code in the future.

The case statement begins with the **case** keyword, followed by the name of the variable to check, and then the **of** keyword. Each possible value is then listed, followed by a colon (:) and the statement to run if that condition is true.

case VariableName of
  possible value : action to carry out;
else
  action to carry out if none of the conditions met;
end;

As with an **if** statement, you can have an optional **else** for when the variable has none of the values.

Each condition can have a block of statements wrapped around a **begin** and **end;** although it may be simpler to put the block of code in a procedure/function!

The **case** statement always has an **end;** at the end.

Boolean Variables

When both the **if** and **case** statements are check values, they are checking whether a condition is true or false.

You can also set a value to a boolean variable by assigning the comparison to that variable, which will then store the result.

For example, if we have code to check whether someone is over 18 (e.g. a shop application to ensure someone can legally buy alcohol) we could check the value as follows:

```
isAge := PersonsAge >= 18;
```

If the persons age is over or equal to 18, then isAge will be set to true – otherwise it will be set to false.

You can then use the value of the **isAge** variable in an **if** statement:

```
if isAge then
   writeln('Can legally buy alcohol')
else
   writeln('They can not purchase alcohol');
```

What if we wish to check that the person is buying alcohol and if they are check their age?

```
BuyingAlcohol := ProductBrought = 'alcohol';
IsAge := PersonsAge >= 18;
if (BuyingAlcohol) and (isAge) then
   writeln('Allow purchase')
else
   writeln('Stop purchase!');
```

The above can be more readable then making the actual comparison in the **if** statement:

```
if (ProductBrought = 'alcohol') and (PersonsAge >= 18) then
   writeln('Allow purchase')
else
   writeln('Stop purchase!');
```

Storing the result of a comparison in a boolean variable can be useful if you need to use that result more then once (although consider whether a function returning a boolean type may be more appropriate!), for example in a nested or multiple if statements.

Operators

You will have seen these operators already in this book, but here is short description of all the operators you can use for comparing values:

=	Equals (i.e. values not the same) – not to be confused with ":=" which assigns a value.
>	Over a particular value.
>=	Over or equal to a particular value.
<	Less then a particular value.
<=	Less then or equal to a particular value.
<>	Does not equal (i.e. both values are not the same).

Looping

There are occasions where you will wish to carry out the same action more then once.

In Pascal there are three ways of doing this: **for**, **while** and **repeat**.

For	Use when you know exactly how many times you wish to run the statements.
While	Use when you don't know how many times a statement will run, or whether it will run at all.
Repeat	Similar to **while**, but the statement will run at least once, until the condition is met.

For

One of the simplest statements for looping is the **for** statements, which runs through the loop a set number of times.

This is useful if you know exactly how many times you wish to run a set of statements.

for VariableName := StartNumber to EndNumber do
carry out statements

With the above, you are setting a value to VariableName, and it changes that value to the current number each time it loops through. StartNumber is the starting number and EndNumber is the end number.

Let's have a look at a very simple example:

```
program ForExample;

var
count:integer;

begin
   for count := 1 to 10 do
      writeln('This is number ',count);
end.
```

You can probably guess my next question (especially if you have read my previous chapters and examples) – can you look at the code and guess what it does?

Answer – it runs through a loop a number of times displaying a number. Obviously this is a very simple example – in a "real world" application you would be doing something more useful while looping!

Type the code in for yourself, and try it out!

```
C:\Documents and Settings\Simon\Desktop\Book Code>forexample
This is number 1
This is number 2
This is number 3
This is number 4
This is number 5
This is number 6
This is number 7
This is number 8
This is number 9
This is number 10
```

As usual, try experimenting with the code, for example...

- Have a block of statements (i.e. between a **begin** and **end;** in the for loop rather then a single statement), perhaps with a running total of the numbers so far!

- In previous sections I've mentioned that sometimes when you have a block of statements it may be more appropriate to move them to a separate procedure or function – try moving the block of code that you wrote above to a separate procedure.

- Store the starting number (1) and ending number (10) in a constant.

- Change the starting number to another number (e.g. 5).

- Store the ending number in a variable, and get the user to input an amount first (e.g. if the user types in 20, it will loop through 20 times).

While experimenting, you might end up with code similar to the following:

```
program ForExample2;

const
StartingNumber = 5;
EndingNumber = 20;

var
count:integer;
Total:integer;

begin
    Total := 0;
```

```
for count := StartingNumber to EndingNumber do
   begin   {for}
      writeln('This is number ',count);
        Total := Total + count;
        writeln('Current total is ',Total);
     end;    {for}
   writeln('Overall total is ',Total);
end.
```

(I've not done all my suggestions, for example moving to a separate procedure, but don't be afraid to try that for yourself)

```
C:\Documents and Settings\Simon\Desktop\Book Code>forexample2
This is number 5
Current total is 5
This is number 6
Current total is 11
This is number 7
Current total is 18
This is number 8
Current total is 26
This is number 9
Current total is 35
This is number 10
Current total is 45
This is number 11
Current total is 56
This is number 12
Current total is 68
This is number 13
Current total is 81
This is number 14
Current total is 95
This is number 15
Current total is 110
This is number 16
Current total is 126
This is number 17
Current total is 143
This is number 18
Current total is 161
This is number 19
Current total is 180
This is number 20
Current total is 200
Overall total is 200
```

Sometimes you may wish to count downwards (i.e. start with a high number, end with a low number) – in which case you would use the **downto** keyword instead of **to**:

for count := HighestNumber downto LowestNumber do
  carry out statements

And here is another example (similar to the first example I gave you – but using **downto** instead of **to**):

```
program ForExample3;

var
count:integer;

begin
   for count := 20 downto 1 do
      writeln('The current number is ',count);
end.
```

And when you run the application:

```
C:\Documents and Settings\Simon\Desktop\Book Code>forexample3
The current number is 20
The current number is 19
The current number is 18
The current number is 17
The current number is 16
The current number is 15
The current number is 14
The current number is 13
The current number is 12
The current number is 11
The current number is 10
The current number is 9
The current number is 8
The current number is 7
The current number is 6
The current number is 5
The current number is 4
The current number is 3
The current number is 2
The current number is 1
```

As with the first example, try modifying the code and experimenting.

One additional hint I will give you – I usually use the variable name of **count** for the variable in the **for** loop (and also the **repeat** and **while** loops where a variable is used to keep count of something). Some developers like to use a variable name with a single letter (e.g. "x") but I find using the name **count** helps make it clear what the variable is for (keeping count), and prevents it being confused with anything else!

Repeat

The **repeat** statement can be used where you wish to loop through a list of statements at least once, until a particular condition is met.

For example, you may wish to use the statement to carry out a search until a match is found, repeat a request for user input until a valid value is entered, or run through a menu and then exit when the user selects the option to exit.

Here's a simple example:

```
program RepeatExample;

var
UsersNumber:integer;

begin
   repeat
      write('Please enter a number between 4 and 10:');
      readln(UsersNumber);
   until (UsersNumber > 4) and (UsersNumber < 10);
end.
```

The above example gets the user to enter a number between 4 and 10, and repeats that request until they enter a valid number.

Type in the code yourself, and run it.

```
C:\Documents and Settings\Simon\Desktop\Book Code>RepeatExample
Please enter a number between 4 and 10:20
Please enter a number between 4 and 10:3
Please enter a number between 4 and 10:10
Please enter a number between 4 and 10:5

C:\Documents and Settings\Simon\Desktop\Book Code>
```

Run it a number of times, entering different numbers – the example only exists when a number between 4 and 10 is entered.

Try modifying the code for yourself:

- Set the numbers 4 and 10 in a constant, and then change them to different numbers.
- Allow the numbers 4 and 10 to be inclusive (hint: use ">=" instead of ">")

If you try my suggestions above, you could end up with something like this:

```
program RepeatExample2;

const
LowestValidNumber = 10;
HighestValidNumber = 25;

var
UsersNumber:integer;

begin
   repeat
      write('Please enter a number between ',LowestValidNumber,'
and ',HighestValidNumber,':');
         readln(UsersNumber);
   until (UsersNumber >= LowestValidNumber) and (UsersNumber <=
HighestValidNumber);
end.
```

And when you run it:

```
C:\Documents and Settings\Simon\Desktop\Book Code>RepeatExample2
Please enter a number between 10 and 25:4
Please enter a number between 10 and 25:9
Please enter a number between 10 and 25:26
Please enter a number between 10 and 25:40
Please enter a number between 10 and 25:1
Please enter a number between 10 and 25:10
```

While

The **while** loop runs and continues to run only if and until a condition is met.

It is different to the **repeat** loop in that it may not run if the condition is not met initially, while the **repeat** loop will always run at least once.

while condition = true do
  carry out statements

Examples of where the **while** loop can be useful include navigating through a file (the file may be empty in which case the loop won't run – more on files later!) or carrying out a search.

An example of using a **while** loop will be included in a later chapter, when we look at files.

Arrays

On occasion you may wish to store a group of data, or store multiple values within a variable – this is possible using arrays.

So far, the variables we have seen are a bit like one storage box:

Arrays allow you to have multiple storage boxes:

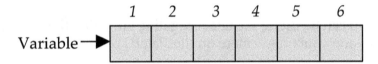

For example, if you have an address book application, you will wish to store multiple names and addresses!

You can declare an array as follows:

```
var
ArrayName:array[1..MaxSize] of ArrayType
```

Where ArrayType is the data type you wish to use (e.g. string, integer, etc.) and MaxSize is the size of the array (you can either use a constant or an actual number).

When using other languages (e.g. C++) be aware that most other languages start their arrays at 0 rather then 1!

Array Sizes

As part of the declaration, you will notice that you have to set the size of the array, i.e. the maximum number of items that can be stored.

You can either enter a number as part of the declaration, for example...

```
var
LotteryNumbers:array[1..6] of integer;
```

or declare a constant and use that constant in your declaration...

```
const
NoOfLotteryNumbers = 6;

var
LotteryNumbers:array[1..NoOfLotteryNumbers] of integer;
```

Accessing values in arrays

To access values in arrays, either to set or read values, use the variable name followed by the position in the array you wish to access within square brackets, for example...

```
LotteryNumbers[1] := 48;
```

would set the first item in the array to 48.

```
writeln(LotteryNumbers[4]);
```

would write the fourth item in the array to the screen.

If you try to access a value beyond the size of the array, you will get a runtime error! For example, if the size of the array is 10 and you try to access item number 11, your application will crash.

Some examples using arrays

This is a somewhat longer example, it stores details of a registration list, and allows you to either add or view the list.

```
program RegistrationList;
{by Simon Pittman
Stores and manages a list of names}

var
theNames:array[1..20] of string;
amount:integer;
UserSelection:shortint;
doExit:boolean;

procedure AddNewName(const NewName:string);

   begin    {procedure}
      amount := amount + 1;
        theNames[amount] := NewName;
   end;    {procedure}

procedure AddToList;

   var
   NewPerson:string;

   begin    {procedure}
      writeln('Enter the new persons name:');
       readln(NewPerson);
       AddNewName(NewPerson);
   end;    {procedure}

procedure DisplayList;

   var
```

```
    count:integer;

  begin    {procedure}
     for count := 1 to amount do
         writeln(theNames[count]);
  end;    {procedure}

procedure AddInitialNames;

  begin    {procedure}
     AddNewName('Simon Pittman');
     AddNewName('Ann Example');
     AddNewName('Joe Bloggs');
  end;    {procedure}

procedure ActOnSelection(const UserSelection:shortint);

  begin    {procedure}
     case UserSelection of
         1 : AddToList;
         2 : DisplayList;
         3 : doExit := true;
     else
         writeln('Not a valid selection');
     end;    {case}
  end;    {procedure}

function DisplayMenu:shortint;

  var
  UserSelection:shortint;

  begin    {function}
     writeln(amount,' names in registration list');
     writeln;    {blank line}
     writeln('1) Add name');
     writeln('2) View registration list');
     writeln('3) Exit');
     write('Your selection:');
     readln(UserSelection);
     DisplayMenu := UserSelection;
```

```
  end;    {function}
begin
   amount := 0;
   AddInitialNames;
   doExit := false;
   repeat
      UserSelection := DisplayMenu;
       ActOnSelection(UserSelection);
   until doExit;
end.
```

You'll notice the above code adds some initial names as well.

As usual type in the example yourself and try it out.

```
C:\Documents and Settings\Simon\Desktop\Book Code>RegistrationList
3 names in registration list

1) Add name
2) View registration list
3) Exit
Your selection:2
Simon Pittman
Ann Example
Joe Bloggs
3 names in registration list

1) Add name
2) View registration list
3) Exit
Your selection:1
Enter the new persons name:
Joe Somebody
4 names in registration list

1) Add name
2) View registration list
3) Exit
Your selection:1
Enter the new persons name:
Glenda Smith
5 names in registration list

1) Add name
2) View registration list
3) Exit
Your selection:2
Simon Pittman
Ann Example
Joe Bloggs
Joe Somebody
Glenda Smith
5 names in registration list

1) Add name
2) View registration list
3) Exit
Your selection:3

C:\Documents and Settings\Simon\Desktop\Book Code>_
```

Try adding names, removing names, etc.

Some things worth noting about the code...

- Particular tasks are split into separate procedures/functions. Particularly worth noting is the **AddNewName** procedure which is used more then once.

- The **amount** variable is used to store the amount of items in the array, useful as not all 20 items in the array are used.

- A menu is displayed and a **case** statement used to determine and carry out the user's desired action.

When running the application, try the following...

- Try adding more then 20 items – what happens?
- Try entering something other then a number when selecting a menu option.

In both the above, the application crashes.

Try modifying the code to include the following...

- Check if the array is full and then display an error. (**HINT:** use a constant to store the number of items in the array, which you use when declaring the array, and then in your code check whether **amount** equals the size of the array to determine whether its full).

- Add an additional menu option to delete an item. How will you select the item to delete? What happens to the missing item in the array (you could either move the last item in the array to replace the deleted item, or move all items after the deleted item down)?

In a "real world" application you would probably sort the list of names... you can have a go at this if you wish – if you do decide to give this a try you may wish to work out how you will do it using a piece of paper first.

More advanced arrays

Its also possible to have **dynamic arrays** – arrays where the size can be changed within the application (rather then a fixed size as used in the previous examples) rather then a fixed size.

Its also possible to have a 2 dimensional array - imagine a grid of storage boxes:

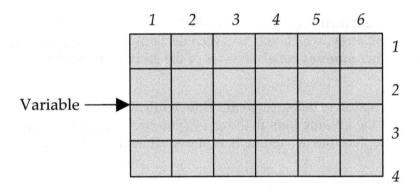

Examples of where a 2 dimensional array can be useful include storing details of a map, or pieces on a chess board.

Both dynamic and 2 dimensional arrays are more advanced topics, which you can learn more about in the future if you wish, but won't be covered here (although still worth knowing they exist).

Type Declaration

In Pascal, the **type** keyword allows you to create your own data type:

```
type
newdatatype = array[1..10] of integer;

var
myvariable:newdatatype;
```

The type declaration goes before your variable declaration section in your code.

In the above example, a data type called **newdatatype** is declared, which is an array of integers. You'll then see that a variable is declared using that new data type.

You could easily create a new data type using an existing variable... here are some examples:

```
const
CharArraySize = 100;

type
{an integer that can only have a value between 1 and 10...}
MiniInteger = 1..10;
{a data type that is the same as an integer...}
IntegerCopycat = integer;
{a string...}
StringCopycat = string;
{an array of characters...}
CharacterArray = array[1..CharArraySize] of char;
```

Some of the above examples are a bit silly (for example, **StringCopycat** and **IntegerCopycat**... we could just as easily use the integer or string data types) but hopefully this gives you an idea of how the data type declaration can work.

From the above examples, you can also see that we can create a data type that is an array, this can make your code more readable, simpler and easier to make changes, especially if you have more then one array.

The last example is very interesting: **CharacterArray** – in older programming languages there was not a string data type, so developers use to have to create their own string data type, which was an array of characters! In fact, the string data type in Pascal is just that – an array of characters (you can even access each individual character in a string, item 0 in the string array stores the length of the string).

In the next chapter, we will look at **records** which make use of the type declaration.

Records

There will be times when you need to group data together, for example names and addresses. This is possible using records.

In the previous section we explored the **type** declaration, and we use this to create a record, for example...

```
type
TAddressDetails = record
   Surname:string[20];
   FirstName:string[20];
   Address:string[40];
   City:string[20];
   end;    {record}
```

You can have variables of any data type within the record, whether they are strings, integers, floating point numbers or even a combination.

You can then declare the record as a variable...

```
var
AddressDetails:TAddressDetails;
```

To access a record in your code, use the name of the record, followed by a full stop and then the name of the record item, for example...

```
AddressDetails.FirstName := 'Simon';
writeln(AddressDetails.City);
```

Using records for your data can also be useful if you wish to save your data to a file – more on this later!

Array of Records

Sometimes you may wish to group data together, and then have more then one record, for example to create an address book application. You can do this by putting the record in an array.

```
Type
TPersonsName = record
   FirstName:string[20];
   MiddleInitial:char;
   Surname:string[20];
   end;    {record}
TPersonArray = array[1..10] of TPersonsName;
```

You can then declare the array as a variable...

```
var
PersonalList:TPersonArray;
```

You can access an item in the array...

```
PersonalList[3].MiddleInitial := 'F';
writeln(PersonList[6].Surname);

for count := 1 to 10 do
   writeln(PersonList[count].FirstName);
```

Opening & Saving Files

Many applications need to save information to files, whether they are settings or documents. This can be a advanced task – this chapter will only provide a brief overview. How you handle files can vary depending on which programming language you are using, and in Pascal which compiler you are using (although they are fairly consistent these days).

When opening and saving files, the logic remains the same...

Associate the file with a variable for handling the file
Read/write data from/to the file
Close the file

There are other advanced considerations, e.g. error checking, checking if the file is open by another application, read only, etc. that will not be covered in this book.

Text Files

As obvious as it sounds, text files contain text. They are the kind of files you create in Notepad, Notepad++ or any other text editor.

They can be useful for storing basic data.

You can declare a text file using **file of Text** or **TextFile** as your data type:

```
var
NamesFile:TextFile;
```

You can read details from the text file, for example:

```
AssignFile(NamesFile,'People.txt');
reset(NamesFile);
while not eof(NamesFile) do
   begin    {while}
      readln(NamesFile,CurrentName);
      writeln(CurrentName);
   end;    {while}
CloseFile(NamesFile);
```

The above example opens a file, "People.txt", which contains a list of names. Each line from the file is read (the **eof** function is used to check when the end of the file is reached and therefore to stop reading the file). The **readln** function includes the internal filename, and a string variable, "CurrentName", which is used to store the name read from file. That name is then written to the screen. At the end, the file is closed using the **CloseFile** statement.

You can also write to files using the **rewrite** statement and **writeln** statements instead of **reset** and **readln**.

Data Files

Data files are good for saving more advanced data. For example, you may wish to save records or sets of data, where writing out each detail line-by-line may not be efficient. Data files can not be opened in a text editor (unlike text files) but can be opened and saved by your application.

To declare a file variable, declare a variable, use the **FILE OF** keyword and the appropriate data type (usually a record).

```
var
PeopleFile:file of TPerson;
```

You can then write details to file:

```
AssignFile(PeopleFile,'AddressBook.dat');
rewrite(PeopleFile);
for count := 1 to amount do
    write(PeopleFile,AddressList[count]);
CloseFile(PeopleFile);
```

The above example goes through an array, writing each entry to file.

The **AssignFile** statement associates the file variable with the actual filename, while the **rewrite** statement prepares the file for writing to (overwriting any previous contents). A **for** statement is then used to write each persons details in the address list to file before it is closed.

Pascal does include an **append** statement, which is similar to the **rewrite** statement except details are added to the end of the file.

If you wish to read a file, you can use the **reset** statement instead:

```
AssignFile(PeopleFile,'AddressBook.dat');
reset(PeopleFile);
count := 1;
while not eof(PeopleFile) do
    begin    {while}
        read(PeopleFile,AddressList[count]);
        count := count + 1;
    end;    {while}
```

The **reset** statement opens the file for reading, while the **eof** function ensures the file is read and details added until the end of the file is reached.

Pointers

Pointers work similarly to variables, but instead of containing data, they merely point to where in memory the data is stored.

When you read that, you probably think it sounds crazy! However, they can be useful, for example you can use pointers to create a list of data where you don't know how many items will be in your list.[3]

You create a pointer by including a ^ in your variable declaration (if you can't find it, on a UK keyboard its what you get when you press SHIFT and 6).

```
type
TPointer = ^integer;

var
VariableName:TPointer;
```

To access a pointer, again use the ^:

```
writeln(^VariableName);
```

---

[3]You could use a **dynamic array** for a list, but it can be useful to learn a bit about pointers. In many implementations of Pascal dynamic arrays actually use pointers in the background.

You can even have records, which contain the location of the next item...

```
type
TNamePointer = ^TNameRecord;
TNameRecord = record
    PersonsName:string;
    NextItem:TNamePointer;
end;
```

You'll notice the rules are being broken a bit – TNamePointer is referring to a data type before its declared! NextItem in the record contains the location of the next item in your list. Pascal allows breaking the rules in this situation.

Pointers can be a very advanced area, however hopefully you'll now have a better understanding of what they are if you wish to (or require) to investigate and learn more about them in the future.

Splitting code into separate files

Code can become quite long – and sometimes it is useful to split your code into separate files, for example you may have the code for your user interface/front end in one file, and the code for your actual logic/processing in another file. Your application can then access and use the code from these files.

These have numerous advantages, including...

- As I've already mentioned, it allows you to keep your user interface (how the user interacts with your application) and the back end workings separate.

- It helps make your code reusable. For example, if you have a procedure or function for connecting to a database, you can use that file containing your code within other applications.

- When working within a team, different team members can develop and test their code independently, with their code being in separate files.

- When files containing code are really really long, it can make it easier to maintain if the code is split into separate files.

Pascal has two ways of using code from other files. The main and frequent method is the **uses** statement.

In Pascal, you can create **units**, which are structured as follows...

```
unit unitname;

interface
```

    Any variables, procedure/function headers that
    are visible outside the file (i.e. can be
    accessed from other files).

```
implementation
```

    Any variables, procedures/functions only
    accessed by the unit and the implementation
    of procedures/functions declared in
    the interface section.

```
end.
```

In the **interface** section you include the declaration of the procedure/function, and then actually code it within the **implementation** section. Units can be compiled separately, but they are not applications, they can only be used by other code files.

You can use a unit in code using the **uses** statement:

```
uses
unitname, unitname;
```

Some implementations of Pascal also allow you to use an "include" declaration that allows you to include code from other files, as if they where part of the same code file (as opposed to units, which treat the different code files as separate items, can be compiled separately and accessed from other files). Some programming languages use this as the main way of splitting code into separate files.

Try Except Finally

Sometimes you may wish to check for errors that are impossible to check or account for using the usual statements, for example errors that occur while opening a file, entering a letter instead of a number, etc.

There are two statements in Pascal – the **try finally** statement and the **try except** statement. These can be used to carry out an action if the application crashes or something happens outwith the application (e.g. within the operating system) causing it to crash.

It should be made clear that these statements are not an alternative for implementing proper error checking within the application.

Imagine them as a safety net – the net is there if the worst happens, but its a last resort rather then the only safety mechanism that you have available!

The **try finally** statement carries out one or more statements, and then always carries out particular actions at the end, even if the application crashes. For example...

```
try
    actions to carry out
finally
    actions that should always be carried out
end;
```

For example, if you open a file, you may wish to use **try finally** to ensure the file always closes, even if the application crashes. Or if creating something that takes up a lot of memory, ensure that the memory is freed at the end, no matter what.

Try except statements can be used to carry out an action, and then carry out a particular action if an exception occurs (i.e. the application crashes, or anything that would produce a runtime error).

```
try
    readln(theNumber);
except
    writeln('That is not a number!');
end;
```

In the **except** section you can specify different actions depending on the type of exception.

The difference between **try except** and **try finally** is that anything in the **except** section only occurs if a runtime error occurs, and anything in the **finally** section is always run, even if the application crashes.

Some programming languages combine both sets of statements into a single statement, for example **try...except...finally**. However in Pascal these are two separate statements, although you can have a **try except** statement nested within a **try finally** statement:

```
try
    try
        actions to carry out
    except
        actions to carry out if there is an error
    end;
finally
    actions to always carry out at end (e.g. closing a file)
end;
```

The **try** statements are more advanced topic, worth knowing they exist and if you want to find out more information is available in documentation, online, etc.

Remember – the **try** statements should not be used as alternatives to proper error checking!

Runtime Library

We have previously looked at splitting code into separate files, one of the advantages being that your code is reusable in different applications that you develop. Many developers have built up a library of code, full of common functions and procedures they use throughout their careers.

Many compilers and language implementations include a runtime library – these are code that have been written to save you time, with functions commonly used by many developers. For example, runtime libraries may include...

- User interface elements, e.g. windows, buttons, etc.
- Common functions like printing, connecting to databases, etc.
- Accessing operating system functions, for example displaying the save dialogues, printing, etc.
- Clearing the screen, displaying text, saving files, accessing the current day and much more.
- Common mathematical calculations.
- Accessing computer networks, graphic cards, sound cards, etc.

This can save you a lot of time – as you don't need to implement the included items yourself.

You can often find documentation for the runtime library, explaining what each item does. You can be very surprised at what is included! Might sound scary, but it is worth looking at the documentation - it can be very surprising to see what is included.

To access code from the runtime library, use the **uses** statement, and include the name of the unit you wish to call.

Let's look at a very simple example:

```
program ClearHello;

uses
crt;

begin
   clrscr;
   writeln('Hello!');
end.
```

The **crt** unit included with Pascal contains functions for text based applications, and in this example we use its **clrscr** procedure to clear the screen!

```
Hello!
C:\Documents and Settings\Simon\Desktop\Book Code>
```

You can also download and obtain libraries of code from other developers, which you can also use and add to your programming library – but make sure you read the license information as they may require you to pay a fee to the developer to use them, be open source, etc.

As I've already mentioned, over time you will probably have your own library of code that can be reused.

Licensing for code in the runtime library included with your compiler will usually be covered by the compiler's license agreement, but be sure to check before using the code within your applications.

Introduction to Data Structures

In this book, we have stored groups of data in an array.

However, imagine you have lots of data, thousands and possibly millions! Going through each piece of data one by one could be inefficient and time consuming for your application, especially if what it is looking for is at the very end of the array.

There are different types of data structures, usually created using pointers. For example there is a tree type structure:

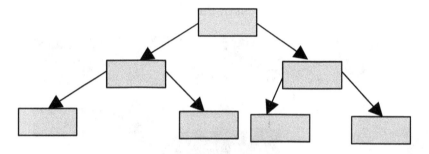

In this tree, data is stored depending on the value of a key field, and therefore searching can be more efficient (I've simplified the above illustration a bit, so it doesn't include any values, pointers, etc.)

Some data structures, for example stacks (only the top item in that data structure can be accessed, removed, etc.) and queues (the item at the front can be accessed, while anything added goes to the back of the queue) exist for various purposes, for example stacks can sometimes be used when developing compilers.

Data structures usually sort data according to the value of a key field.

Some developers create data structures and make these available for other developers to use with their application data, some compilers and development tools even include these with their runtime library so you don't need to implement them yourself.

This book will not go into any great detail or include example code, as these are more advanced topics, but as with some other advanced topics I've covered, it is worth knowing that they exist, and you can find out more if you wish.

Resolving Errors & Runtime Errors

Compiler Errors

You've just written a piece of code, compiled it and then get a list of compiler errors – your code has not compiled! The first few times it happens, it can seem daunting, but remember even the most experienced developers still get errors when writing their code.

You may just get one error, two errors or a whole list of them!

```
C:\Documents and Settings\Simon\Desktop>fpc vatcalculator.pas
Free Pascal Compiler version 2.6.2 [2013/02/12] for i386
Copyright (c) 1993-2012 by Florian Klaempfl and others
Target OS: Win32 for i386
Compiling vatcalculator.pas
vatcalculator.pas(16,19) Error: Identifier not found "ItemPric"
vatcalculator.pas(17,15) Warning: Variable "ItemPrice" does not seem to be initi
alized
vatcalculator.pas(21,4) Fatal: Syntax error, ";" expected but "identifier WRITEL
N" found
Fatal: Compilation aborted
Error: C:\FPC\2.6.2\bin\i386-Win32\ppc386.exe returned an error exitcode (normal
 if you did not specify a source file to be compiled)
```

First of all, don't panic!

Don't try to solve all the errors you see at the same time.

Start by looking at the first error in the list, and try to fix that error. Once you've fixed it try compiling the code again – **don't try solving any of the other errors in the list**.

With a bit of luck, you'll have solved the error in the top of the list. You can then continue to work your way down the list of errors, solving the error at the top of the list and compiling your code.

Chances are that the error at the top of the list may have caused some of the other errors you got further down.

The compiler will display the line number and the name of the code file where the error occurs, so it should be easy to identify the line of code that has the error! Read the cause of the error given by the compiler, as it will tell you what is causing the compiler to produce an error.

Frequent causes of errors can include...

- A missing semicolon at the end of a line.

- A **begin** without an **end** (this is when indenting code can be really useful for identifying these kind of errors).

- Opening a bracket without closing the bracket, or closing a bracket an extra time! For example **writeln('Hello';** or **writeln('Hello'));**

- Mis-spelling a variable name.

- Getting variable names mixed up and using the wrong variable for something.

- Trying to change the value of a constant.

If your code has compiled but produced a list of warnings and notes, do check these lines of code as well, while your code will still compile these warnings or hints can be possible causes of runtime errors (more on this in the next section).

Runtime Errors & Causes

The most annoying thing that can happen is when you run an application, and it crashes, most often with a "runtime error".

Why does the compiler not pick up these errors while compiling? Well the compiler may think your code is working and error free, and therefore compile it anyway. For example, it could be an impossible calculation, a variable that does not have a value, etc.

Sometimes your compiler will display warnings or hints - keep an eye out for these, the code will still compile, but the compiler is warning you that there may be problems. If you ever get hints, notes or warnings, do have a look at your code – even if the application is running as expected, paying attention to the warnings can help ensure there are no errors or problems in the future.

```
C:\Documents and Settings\Simon\Desktop>fpc vatcalculator.pas
Free Pascal Compiler version 2.6.2 [2013/02/12] for i386
Copyright (c) 1993-2012 by Florian Klaempfl and others
Target OS: Win32 for i386
Compiling vatcalculator.pas
vatcalculator.pas(15,21) Warning: Variable "ItemPrice" does not seem to be initi
alized
vatcalculator.pas(12,1) Note: Local variable "ItemName" not used
Linking vatcalculator.exe
21 lines compiled, 0.1 sec , 32368 bytes code, 1868 bytes data
1 warning(s) issued
1 note(s) issued
```

Possible causes of runtime errors can include...

- Variables not being initialised, i.e. they do not have a value. For example, you could be attempting to display the value of a variable, but not actually given it a value!

- Carrying out an impossible calculation, for example dividing a number by zero.

- When there is a **readln** statement, entering a word when the user should be entering a number!

If you can't spot the cause of a runtime error, try the following...

- Look at your code, and using a piece of paper follow the steps on paper and see what is happening – trying out the steps in your head, noting down any values to variables, etc.

- Add a temporary **writeln** statement before and after statements you suspect are causing the problem, to help identify which lines of code are causing the problem.

- Some compilers include additional options to identify the line number of where the runtime error is occurring. In FreePascal, you can compile your code using the **-gl -gh** options, for example **fpc -gl -gh vatcalculator.pas** – when a runtime error occurs the error will display the line number.

Unexpected Results

When you run an application, especially while testing, unexpected results may occur, and you have to go back to your code and see what is happening and causing the unexpected result.

The best thing to do is sit down with a piece of paper, and go through your code line-by-line, carrying out the action in your head and noting down the values of variables as they change.

You may wish to include additional statements while identifying the problem displaying data/additional information, e.g. a value up to that point, to ensure anything before that line of code is being run properly and what the current values are.

Also check calculations carefully where appropriate, to make sure the calculations are correct – the simplest and smallest mistake can sometimes cause the biggest problems.

Sometimes an unexpected result can occur because you are entering an unexpected value (remember to test code by entering values that you would never expect your user to enter – because chances are someone will enter that value) – for example if prompting the user for a number between 1 and 10, what happens when the user enters 0 or 11? Or types in a word? Remember to include error checking in your application, and try to cover all possibilities!

Tips & Tricks

Global/Local variables

One good tip I've always learned is to always try to avoid using global variables – where possible variables should be declared locally within a procedure/function.

This can help reduce the amount (and risk) of errors within your code, as only that procedure/function can read and make changes to that variable.

If the variable is used in other procedures/functions then you could consider using parameters instead, and passing the local variable to that procedure/function that way. In parameters, remember you can also determine whether that parameter is read only (using the **const** keyword) and therefore reducing the risk of errors further if appropriate.

Each time you declare a global variable, ask yourself whether it can be a local variable within a procedure/function?

Planning and designing on paper

It can be very tempting to just go to your computer, and start writing code immediately.

However, it does make sense to plan what you are going to do on paper first.

If you are creating a user interface, sketch and draw what it looks like on paper.

When writing code, think about the logic and how its going to do things – when you do this more often then not you will find your code is more efficient!

There are a range of methods for designing your code on paper – flow charts can be a popular visual method. You can also write pseudocode, which is the logic in an English form rather then a programming language, for example....

Declare theName as a string variable
Prompt user to enter their name
Get user to enter their name and store value in theName
Display a hello message to the user using theName

This can be especially useful when carrying out calculations.

When using flow charts or pseudocode, go through your code on paper, test any calculations and steps, including for possible errors that your user may make.

Designing your code on paper is a good way of breaking your application down into smaller steps, and different procedures/functions.

Structure & Indentation

Throughout this book (and any examples of code you see elsewhere) you will notice my code is structured and indented – this helps make the code more clearer and readable.

Different organisations have different standards and preferences when it comes to indentation and layout of code (and can even publish their own guidelines/policy), however the most important thing is to be consistent.

In my examples, I have 3 spaces of any code between a **begin** and **end** and also that follow any other statement (e.g. **if, repeat**, etc.).

```
begin
   writeln('What is your name?');
   readln(theName);
   if theName = 'Simon' then
      writeln('You have the same name as the developer!');
end;
```

Testing

All the code you write should be thoroughly tested, including testing for what happens when there are unexpected situations. You may know that the user is not meant to enter a number over zero when prompted for a number, but there is a good chance someone will enter exactly that value!

Test what happens when the user enters each possible value, and also find out what happens when the user enters a value they are not meant to! If the application crashes, you may need to amend your code to include more error checking.

Don't rush testing, and as brutal as it sounds, try to break your own code/application!

When working in a team and writing a different part of an application or code, test the code you have written. Obviously in this situation you may not have access to the other application code, so create a small test application to test your code. In a team environment, if can also be helpful to get other members of your team to test your code as well, to see if they manage to break it.

Its better that you (or other members of your development team) break your own code, rather then the application crashing or producing unexpected results when being used by someone using your software.

Keeping your user interface/logic separate

Another good practice I've been taught is to keep your user interface (what the user sees and how they interact with the application) and the code/logic separate.

Not only does this allow the front end (the user interface) to be developed separately from the back end (the code that gets the application to do stuff), but it also helps make your code more reusable. For example, code written for a desktop application could be reused for a web, mobile or text based application.

If a procedure/function in the back end checks for errors, rather then displaying an error you could have a boolean variable (as a parameter) that is returned as **true** if there is an error, the front end can then check the boolean value, and if it indicates there was an error stop and carry out an appropriate action (e.g. displaying an error message).

An entire book could be written on this (and many of the other topics in this chapter) but still worth considering and having in mind when designing and writing applications.

Variable/Constant names

I've seen some developers use a single letter for the name of a variable or constant – try to use meaningful names for variables/constants. This helps make your code more readable. For example, if asking someone for their name and storing in a variable, **PersonsName** is a more sensible name for a variable then **n**.

When deciding a variable name, don't use a name that is also a keyword or the name of a procedure/function otherwise your code won't compile, and it could get messy. If in doubt, I always put the word "the" at the start of a variable name just to be sure, e.g. **theRecord** instead of **Record** for a variable name will avoid the inevitable errors from using the same name as a keyword!

When to use constants

Constants can be very useful, some situations where you may wish to use them...

- Setting the size of an array – it makes it easier to change the size of the array in future, checking whether an array is full, etc.

- String values, for example error messages, using a constant (especially in a graphical application) can make the display of messages much clearer.

- Storing the maximum amount of something.

- Values that are or may be used more then once.

- Numbers used in a calculation.

If a number or value is hard coded into your code (i.e. its not a variable name, but an actual value) a constant may be more appropriate in that situation.

Getting & Finding Help/Info

There is a range of help and further information available if you get stuck, or just want to learn a bit more about a particular area. The most obvious source of help is the Internet, but there is also documentation and books available.

Compiler/RTL documentation

Many compilers come with documentation, explaining what the various options are – don't worry if it seems complex when you first look at it though. If you are using third party code, or a compiler with its own run time library (code with functions that you can use) there will often be documentation or help explaining the functions in the run time library, what it does, how to use, etc.

If you can't see any obvious links to the documentation, it may be stored in the same folder as the compiler or code files. Some vendors also have their documentation available as a separate download or online only on their website.

Development Tools Help

Many development tools include help, not only explaining the various features of your development tools, but explaining statements and functions, what they do and how they work. They may also include examples helping to illustrate how they work.

As with other documentation, if its not installed with the development tools, it may be included as an option in the installation package, or be available online.

Websites

The Internet is a very popular source of information and seeking help – if you are not sure how to do something, typing in the language and what you are trying to do in your search engine (e.g. Google) will often produce search results with the solution.

If you have had a problem, chances are someone else has also asked your question.

A popular website for asking software development/coding questions is Stack Overflow. There are other forums – but if posting a question on a website or forum, be sure to read their rules and forum guidelines first.

Developers of software development tools will often have their own websites, with further information, documentation and sources of help. They may also have their own forums, providing support and allowing you to receive help from other developers using those tools.

You may also find websites and videos online explaining different techniques and skills.

When looking at answers to your problem online, it is often tempting to just copy and paste code, but do take time to actually learn what its doing and then try producing the solution yourself rather then just copying and pasting.

Books

There are many books covering software development – some of them are aimed at beginners, while others cover advanced topics. Different books cover different languages, techniques and tools, and there is a good chance that a book is available covering something you wish to learn about.

Taking your skills further

Graphical Applications

Throughout this book we have written text applications that run on a command line – this has allowed us to focus on the logic and software development, without getting distracted by designing nice user interfaces!

However many applications are graphical applications, for example your office applications, text editors and games.

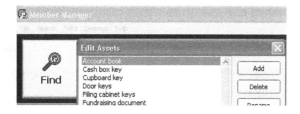

If you intend to develop graphical applications, you may wish to learn about...

- User interface design.

- Keeping the logic for your graphical user interface/display and the inner workings of the application separate so your code can be reused.

- Look at other applications, and see how they are designed and their layout.

Some development tools, including Visual Studio, Delphi and Lazarus, include "form designers", which allow you to create and design a user interface, then write code to get different parts of the application working. Alternatively, you may code your user interface from scratch.

Web Applications

Another popular form of application (especially in recent years) are web applications. You may have heard of the term "cloud" to describe applications that run over the web.

Rather then applications being installed on each computer, the application is stored on a server, perhaps at the application developer's offices, which users of the application then access through a web browser on their computer. They are essentially websites that you then access and use.

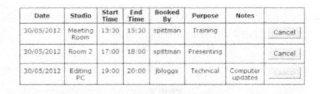

When the user interacts with the application, the server will process the user's action and then return the results to their web browser.

There are a lot of office applications, accounting packages and more that now run on the web rather then being installed on the user's computer.

If you are interested in developing web based application's you may wish to learn the following languages and technologies...

- ASP.NET and C#
- PHP
- JavaScript
- Java

Mobile Development

If you are interested in developing applications for mobile phones and devices, you will probably like to learn...

- Java (for Android phones)
- Swift (for iPhones)

Previously to develop applications for iPhones, Apple used the ObjectiveC language.

You'll probably want to learn more about the operating systems and devices (iOS, Android, Windows Phone, etc.). It can also be helpful to learn about designing user interfaces for phones, as they will have smaller and different screen sizes.

Other languages

Throughout this book, we have used Pascal. If you study or work in software development, there is a good chance that you will learn and use other languages.

You'll find that the structure and basic ideas that you have learned in Pascal can be applied to other languages. Let's compare the hello application with a C++ version as an example.

First, here's the Pascal version from earlier in the book:

```pascal
program SayHello;
{by Simon Pittman
Displays a personalised hello message to the user.}

var
UsersName:string;

begin
   write('What is your name?');
   readln(UsersName);
   writeln('Hello ',UsersName,'!');
end.
```

And now let's look at a version of the same application written in C++...

```cpp
#include<iostream>

using namespace std;

/*
by Simon Pittman
Displays a personalised hello message to the user.
*/
```

```
int main()
{
    string UsersName;
    cout << "What is your name?";
    getline(cin,UsersName);
    cout << "Hello " << UsersName << "!";
}
```

You will see some differences between the C++ and Pascal versions, looking at the code can you identify those differences? However where there are differences you will also notice similarities.

In particular the differences between the code in the two languages are:

- C++ does not include a **program** line.

- Variables are declared within the "begin" and "end" statements rather then outwith. In fact you don't even need to declare variables at the start of the method, you can declare them anywhere else in the block of statements if you wish!

- Instead of **begin** and **end** C++ uses curly brackets { and }

- As you've probably guessed, curly brackets aren't used for comments (they are used for begin and end as already mentioned) – instead you can either use /* **This is a comment** */ or // **This is a comment**

- You will notice the top two lines, the **include** and **using** – these allow you to use code from other files and the namespace part allows you to specify which set of code you are using.

Hopefully once you have learned one language, it is much easier to apply those skills and understanding to help you learn other languages.

Training/Education

If you are interested in pursuing a career in software development, chances are you may plan to study for relevant qualifications at school, college or university and take your skills further, and get officially recognised qualifications! This could be to find employment, or even for something to do in your spare time.

Some colleges and universities not only run fill time courses, but may also offer part time or evening classes in software development – handy if you have other commitments, work, family, etc. or learning just for fun. If you are claiming state benefits, are unemployed, etc. then some places may even offer their courses at a discount or for free – no harm in contacting your local college to find out!

Self Teaching

You could also teach yourself new skills and take things further, whether its by reading other software development books, watching online videos demonstrating different concepts or visiting software development websites/blogs that go into more detail.

Working in Software Development

The starting salary for a junior developer can be £20,000 with the most experienced developers earning around £50,000. At the time of writing (September 2015) many of the jobs advertised include and look for the following...

- A degree or relevant qualification.
- C#
- Java
- Visual Studio
- Eclipse
- SQL
- PHP
- JavaScript
- MySQL
- Sharepoint
- .NET
- Oracle
- C++

This includes developing and maintaining applications for desktops (e.g. Windows and Apple Macs), mobile devices (e.g. Android, iPhone and Windows Phone) and the web.

You've reached the end of the book

That's it, you've reached the end of the book!

Hopefully software development is not as scary as you first thought. Either that or this book has scared you away completely!

As I have said throughout the book, do not be afraid of experimenting! Try creating your own little applications from what you've learned, and modify the examples you've worked on and seen within this book.

You may not be an expert, and you probably won't be creating the next million pound application, but hopefully you have a better idea of what's involved, and have a good starting point if you wish to learn more.

Good luck!

Also by the author

Editing Audio Using Audacity
2013
Whether you are new to editing audio or have used similar software packages, this book will get you started in using Audacity to edit your audio, and point you in the right direction to finding further information and help.

Managing a WordPress Website
2014
If you are responsible for the day to day management and updating of a WordPress website, this book will help you learn and use the different features you need. With less technical detail and more emphasis on managing an existing WordPress website, this book covers editing pages, posting blogs, keeping the WordPress software up-to-date and much more!